SEARCHING FOR ANGELS

ALSO BY LANA ORPHANIDES

Sea and the Sound of Wind, Poems of Greece
Spring: Rebirth and Renewal (a collaborative work)

SEARCHING FOR ANGELS

Poems by

Lana Orphanides

*To Amanda,
Wishing angels
for you!
Lana*

Antrim House

Simsbury, Connecticut

Library of Congress Control Number: 2014922636

ISBN: 978-1-936482-80-1

First Edition, 2015

Printed and bound by Mira Digital Publishing

Book design by Rennie McQuilkin

Line drawings and front cover watercolor by the author

Author photograph by Bruce Hostetler

Antrim House
860.217.0023
AntrimHouse@comcast.net
www.AntrimHouseBooks.com
21 Goodrich Road, Simsbury, CT 06070

To my mother, Jean Claire Tuttle Palmer,

who is in all my poems

ACKNOWLEDGMENTS

Grateful acknowledgment to the editors of the following publications, in which some of the poems in this volume first appeared, at times in earlier versions: *A Letter Among Friends, Southeast Gale,* and *Freshwater.*

Throughout the years I have had encouragement and support from friends, family, and teachers, many of whom will never know the gifts they have given me. I am so grateful to each one. Most important, though, is my husband, Dimi, who has always honored each poem I have written. Among those dear friends who have guided me along the way are my longtime partners and mentors in poetry, Edwina Trentham and Gaynell Meij. Thanks also to Pam Gordinier, with whom I have collaborated on many amazing projects initiated by her, along with our pal, L'Ana Burton. I must also thank my sons who are my true gurus, and their families who are my inspiration.

Finally, special thanks to Pat O'Brien, who said, "Why don't you have a book?" and suggested I send along some poems for consideration by her editor and publisher, the amazing Rennie McQuilkin.

TABLE OF CONTENTS

III. THE PROBLEM OF ETERNITY

IV. HOW MANY MORE WORLDS

V. TWELVE MOONS

VI. WHAT GIVES THE HEART EASE

"The world is indeed full of peril, and in it there are many dark places; but still there is much that is fair, and though in all lands love is now mingled with grief, it grows perhaps the greater."

– *The Two Towers,* J.R.R. Tolkien

SEARCHING

FOR

ANGELS

The Beginning of a Story

The petals of the weeping cherry tree
are finishing their secret life.
They fall
around me like a net and I become a walking garden
leaping bare
foot through the rooted door.
Come with me. You can return.

Inside your mother waits, inside your child
will be born, inside bread is baking,
dawn is glistening,
inside your father dies,
a child falls, one loses hope,
a world is burning, a world is gleaming,
a heart is breaking.

Inside gold birds fly upward.
There is a gravel road and it is filled with sheep.
There is a swaying bridge and at its end,
a waterfall.
Inside you take a ferry boat.
Inside there is the blood of angels,
the first dream and the last.

I have woken as from a sleep
to the heron flying in the early dark,
the fisherman hauling his boat,
the sweet breaths of pine,
the moving gentle clouds,
the soft rise of the hill.

Walk through the door.
Come with me.

I. THE SEEDS WITHIN

Cairn

I was here
under the same blue skies
in the sometime rain.
I was here by the river bed
though I did not see you.
I was here
on the simple path,
in the dust, on the same journey
though you did not see me.

The Seeds Within

You walked across the grass at twilight and the curve
of the earth changed.
The strength of your stride, the force
of your gaze, beguiled me,
the world from which you came unknown,
the world that I had known, gone.

The seeds
of our lives
were in that moment
that we met,
the seeds of our children
and their children,
hidden deep within like sleeping seraphim.

You walked across the grass at twilight
and I, on the opposite side,
saw the curve of the earth shift.

In the angle of that light, we traced a triangle to meet
as if we knew the way,
as if it all was known,
and all
that was to to be
began.

Green

I remember the grass
green in the darkness
and underneath
the giving ground

the lilt of the highway
the waiting car by the side of the road
his soft breath the green stains
on my white skirt

and the sound
it could have been horns
or it could have been us
caroling in the grass

The Vow

How brave we were to marry in the fall
with darkness coming early and the cold
rising from the damp leaves, the sun stalled,
scattered, its wan light no longer gold.

From those years of parting and receding
here we were, in bright sunlight after all,
still daring to go forward, offering, needing
to trust in one quick act, a single vow.

We held tall candles, wore the wedding crowns,
walked a circle as if to cast a spell
tethered by a ribbon, three times round,
tethered by the light, the sound of bells,

the rings, the kiss, the flowers in my hair,
and suddenly gardenias filled the singing air.

Heartbeats

This morning I looked at the two chairs facing each other
under the canopy out of the rain,
imagined the mail coming with his name.

Tonight I count his heartbeats;
the light from the white alarm clock
shines in the darkness, its green numbers
marking the seconds.
I touch the soft silk of his thigh,
throw my arm around his broad, strong back and press
my chest to listen
but I lose count.

Outside the clouds gather in the Florida heat.
The air conditioner sounds like rain.
Each time it starts he jumps in sleep
like one walking unknown terrain.
His feet dance in intervals like skipping rocks
or as if he is crossing a swaying bridge.

In my dreams we are fording a bright river.
We are light
and laughing
and no one is counting.

Invincible

I fold my arms around you,
my smaller body as protection
keeping your bones strong, your skin taut,
swaddling you back to sleep –
the two of us invincible
lying on our sides in the warm bed
while statues of snow cover
all that we know.

A fallacy of course,
the Henry Moore sculptures
and our invincibility, yet
you sleep and so do I
while outside the gray sky
brings more snow,
layer upon layer this winter,
more beautiful
for what is hidden,
for what will not die.

The Night Before the Baby's Birth

Surely by this weekend we will have
a new soul on this earth opening
its eyes to sunlight, to the incredibly blue
eyes of its mother
and its father. It will hear its first
unmuffled sound, breathe spring air,
know the wind of hummingbirds,
and the cool breeze of the shade tree,
learn of balance and space that is not liquid,
learn that it cannot
float in air, feel the soft vitreous womb,
no longer, never again alone,
finding what it is to touch
and the very grandness of that gesture
when one finger locks upon another.

First Born

The body does not forget.
It remembers the child in the belly,
the first feeling of roundness,
the bold corner of a foot,
the milk spilling in the breast.

It stretches and folds and grows
limp. Rises and tightens and grasps
and lets go but does not forget.

Once I watched the birth of a calf as it
struggled out of its mother, she licking
and cleaning and the calf raggedly standing
just out of the womb, falling, resting, rising
once again. The mother too rising quickly
after this hoof-kicking, long-legged birth,
prodding and watching, no lying down, no dreaming.

You too had long legs when you were born
though I hardly remember your coming out,
and I was not standing soon after
but you were clean and fresh as porcelain
and, in the peace of the dark room,
I felt that I was the one
who had come through
to the other side.

The World in Which I Love You

for Elias and Anna

In the world in which I love you
sea chimes ring
and the sounds of birds glitter in the morning air.
The garden fills with purple heather
and the water ripples like delphiniums.
In the world in which I love you no bombs explode,
no one takes his life and no one takes another's.
You sing for half the day,
the god within you like a golden lily.
Angels whisper in your ears.

When you awaken, dreams have sipped your tears.
Banners of peace fly over red grasses
and a hand to hold is lasting.

Star

When Anna was three
she had never seen a star,
did not know the word,
did not know yet
how the calling of things
brings them into being,
that the colors of the rain
or swaths of light across
the midnight sky
are names.
So she asked, "What are stars?"
her deep blue eyes
under their layer
of quizzical lashes
always ready
to ask what she did not know,
seeing
what was false,
observing like the quiet wolf
who, in that painting of the North
where the Northern Lights quiver,
sees with a clear eye
the whole sky before him.

Some Babies

for Elias

Some babies when they are are born
lie on the birth table with arms crossed
over their tiny chests, protective and wary
of the new air and stark light.
You lay with your arms outspread as if you saw
the world welcoming you.

This morning in the gray unnatural cold
of May, a great white heron rose from the creek
spreading its white wings wide
and flew up against the rain.

Summer Afternoon

Sometimes the heart
is pressed down
to overflowing,
trampled in joy
and afraid,
so shaken by love
it is hard
to breathe.

II. VISITATIONS

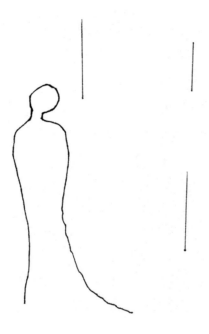

Dad

Last night in sleep I heard my father's words,
the ones he said the day he married late
in life, his face a shining mirror then
to his bride's smile, as though unheralded,
silver angels had suddenly appeared.
In a quiet, gentle voice he said,
"We're going to kiss good night each night," as if
he'd found that golden bough, the answer to it all.

Suddenly awake I saw his long
and distant loneliness, his boyish fly-boy face,
and knew: my mother, full of grace,
sought solitude, a choice he'd never make,
her silence just a state of mind not his.
No answer to how we become someone
that others form, but I held on to his
midnight wings, the message from him that night.

No blame, just truth, balm in a winter dream,
his voice, his rosary-holding star, beaming.

The Artist Paints Palms

Father, let me see your hand
gone past me now.
Was it clear like you and singing?
Did you have within your palm
a tangled path, rivers crossing?

Was my mother's hand
two journeys, a willow in the midst?
Were there hummingbirds
or swordsmen, flying through those fingers
much like mine?

And if our palms could touch
and time slip through like water
in a color much like winter
would I know your sorrows
and its branches?
Would you
know mine?

Your Hair, Mine

for Debbie

The day after your death I cut my hair,
unaware of the tradition of ancient mourners
but thinking somehow to honor you, begin anew,
or, become someone who had not been there

when you died, looking just as you did before, only
surprised by death's swiftness against such a warrior.
But I am changed as if passed through a sieve.
Each molecule, crust of skin, shard of bone altered.

I would weave wisps of your hair into mine,
take your kindness and your strength, carry them
into battle and fly like the great gray
hawk who visited me unexpected

this morning as I sat among your things
listening to the earth and the sweet grass sing.

The Yellow Chair

The yellow chair
under the blue pear tree,
having found she was no longer
of use
at the table,
is building a nest in her lap,
a bower
of golden trumpet flowers
and twining heart shaped leaves
where once only
woven grasses had been.

How You Visit

Sometimes, I hear your laughter in my own,
bubbling up from an underground
spring of sweet water, a trilling sound of a bird
I cannot name unless perhaps

it's a crowd of scarlet tanagers,
or that towhee-like bird
I heard in New Zealand
whose notes were impossibly high and clear,

singing, "Drink your tea, drink dear,"
the last sounds clinking as I climbed
to the Cathedral in the Rock.
But, I don't know.

You do not appear
in my mirror, your hands in their usual movements
of larks flying. It is as though we visit
for a short while but there is no conversation.

That you come in laughter amazes me
and after, I turn my head, sure
of the disappearing scent of your perfume,
and speech, then, seems too tied to earth.

The Dream of Missing You

Running through the theater
I look frantically for you.
Everyone is asking, "Where's she going?
What's she lost?"

Up a staircase
I wind myself into a loft
to find things you might have used,
paints, brushes, empty canvases
white
and flying things,

pottery, gray clay
and on a chair
a soft wool scarf
of browns and golds
the colors of purple finches.

Then, an open window,
bougainvillea,
shining jade, hibiscus,
in a shadowed light of leaves, but
no one's there.

Down the stairs and through the rows of chairs
I whirl again. Behind the seats I find

soft gloves, high-heels, a hairpin, left behind.
Are you somewhere
walking barefoot in the wind?

The room becomes a silent ballroom,
angels on the ceiling, curling columns, grand French doors.
I sit waiting like a child for ballet class to begin.
You should be here, your pile of papers on your lap,
watching me become a star.

Going In

Lavender and the soft haze
of sage, pale green capers,
and wild thyme
lined the path
to the sea. Below us

the beach
was a small, empty crescent,
far from the town,
the moonscape of mountains behind.

The weather was windy, and this our first swim
in the still cold Aegean.
I invited my mother,
dead then eight years, for the dip.

I asked if she'd like to dive with me,
warm me, sustain me, make me look brave.
She smiled, almost laughed
and gladly came diving.

Weightless,
all spirit, her long
swimmer's body
joined mine. Motion and essence,
we arched like a dolphin,
a sound wave
of coming and going.

In that moment as light

rolled into darkness,
ocean spilled into ocean, I was liquid and flowing,
I was past and present, future and never.
I was water and space and the taste
of salt. I was gone
and come back unafraid.

Last Poem

So sit with me here for the last poem.
   Let our eyes
      connect, deep as the heron and the fish.
Don't wander. Sit with me
   and listen
         though
              I have nothing new to tell.
The mockingbird still sings its crazy
   numberless tunes.
           The sea
still holds the fisherman
   with his orange shirt
      in his small hopeful
         boat.
The full moon still
   lingers over the porch, and you
      with your shards of misplaced
         hair –
hold my hand and listen
   as the breath
         of bells
leaves my mouth and the green
   of your eyes
      is my last sight.

When My Mother Was My Age

That sail tall, slim in the wind,
going up or coming down?
Now the boat moves slowly
out it seems, toward the open sea.
When my mother was my age
she had 12 more years to live.
Yesterday a friend died at 66,
surprised.
What do I have to say to you
before I go, before you go?

The sun hovers in the heavy sky,
neither in nor out,
sparkle on the water gone.
The grand canyon, how does it feel
to be there, to whisper into it?
We said we'd go. We must.

III. THE PROBLEM OF ETERNITY

The Problem of Eternity

So it is in my memory a yellow bus
not with wings or lights or large books
or bathrooms or seat belts,
but where the conversation took place.
We were young and smart
in the way innocence
and pensiveness
are smart
and questioning –
of belief, eternity, the universe –
when I decided, silently
or maybe not, that yes,
there is a cosmic spirit,
not a father God or goddess
or priest or pope or queen,
but some force of dual nature,
both face and universe,
some energy of magnificent
molecules, beneficent, angelic,
who left the details to us.
What was lost then?
Many angels, the blessings of Mary
and her prayers, abundant grace?
What was gained:
the universe expanded
then flew open
as we talked through
winter twilight
in the dusty bus of slipping time
and we faced each other boldly
in varying degrees of wonder,
having solved the problem of eternity.

Higgs Boson

And so there comes
the "God particle"
to ignite the mind like Ahab's ocean –
what might be the beginning, before the big bang,
before electrons and protons and neutrons,
before newtons and ergs, before anything
could be measured or weighed or weighed down
or lifted or floated or faded.

Before love
and mountains
and the ever constant horseshoe crab, before
the feet of angels and domes of churches,
before chambers and pyramids
and ostriches and comets, before ice
and hydrogen and carbon and, yes,
love,

there was this: a footprint, a shadow,
a first cause perhaps,
a thing of perfect symmetry,
that, when broken,
creates.

Thirteen Billion Years

For thirteen billion years
the light has been coming.
The Hubble telescope can see
the seeds of the great galaxies.

What next I wonder?
To see the Big Bang itself
and then perhaps
the face
of God, circular and shining

bigger than all the galaxies combined,
a beard of straight starlight, arms extended
beyond the universe
banging on his magnificent drum.

The Conversation

I said, God, where the hell are you?
and God said,
Wait,
I will
appear
blue
and yellow.
I will be square
sometimes
or perhaps oval with rippling edges.
I will be sometimes two parts or many.
I will melt magenta into white paper
and sparkle
or
disappear.
I will be
bubbles in the air or
molecules you cannot see.
I will be waiting
behind that blade of grass.

What Is Seen, What Is Not Seen

The middle of August now,
the Dormition of Mary
quietly sleeping into heaven,
doubting Thomas returning
to catch her girdle thrown
down from above – then he believed.
We didn't catch the meteor showers either,
the Leonids, didn't try, too much effort.
One wonders were they truly there –
were stars flashing in the night sky,
clanging in motion against all the darkness,
naked energy slipping back to earth
and we just not listening?

Heaven

Imagine heaven is a *Star Trek* replay
in colors of brown and gray with crisp uniforms
and smart talk, where an occasional speaking being
eventually fades into empty cosmos
and all the time Captain Kirk longs
for earth.

In his mind silver grass lingers at dawn,
and the orange moon appears above the darkening green
of summer trees. A yellow butterfly,
sure only in its search for blossoms, kindles by.
He dreams of floating on his back,
eyes closed, the sound of rippling water
pulling against the heavy, soft bellied earth.

The Journey

There was something in the sky
a light for sure
no voice that we could recognize
still it drew us
We were waiting for a sign
We could not explain why we gathered those things
why we left that night
when it was so cold for a journey
There was no path
no sure direction
only light
We were tired certainly
tired of where we had been
what we had done with our lives
Time seemed to shorten
to compress and the only sound
our breathing
Occasionally we talked
Each word formed had more meaning
than the usual chatter
There was that light
that lifted something in our spirits
We all agreed
it made us stronger
not thinking of the end of the journey itself
but of this going

The Annunciation

Surely it wasn't Gabriel
the archangel but Gabriella
spiriting through the window,
sitting close beside her
like a mother
or a sister helping make the bread,
spreading out the woven blue of cloth
in the dark, cool kitchen
among the hanging rosemary and the rue

and Mary tying on her sandals,
gathering her thoughts for what
no man could understand
but this angel,
whose message
came like wind
or blowing sand
across a distant desert
like a startling light.

Yet she could not see
the sorrow.
The angel did not tell.

Later would be time enough.

In Broad Daylight

So yesterday I forgot to be grateful
and in the morning I also forgot
to say a joyful mantra.
Today I am waiting for the archangel
to deliver a message of gladness:
Behold! Behold!

I go in search of lilacs quickly,
as they disappear like rain.
I run towards the beach
over broken glass
from the last storm
and I find them. I want to keep them
alive and fresh and bursting with bloom.
I kneel like Gabriel in the Botticelli painting,
his hands it seems in supplication,
her hands saying no, no, as she backs
away.

But the lilacs come into my hands with one
snap. I know I am a thief. They are not
mine to take or keep. In the painting
Gabriel offers Mary a lily.
She takes it, even as it withers in her hand.

IV. HOW MANY MORE WORLDS

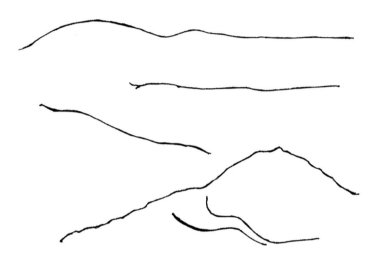

Her Other Name

When she was Gabriella Orvieto
she soared and flew. Her eyes were bright and clear.
She knew each glance, the way to trick the fear,

what looks would kill, what words say no.
The girl had no regrets, each road was new.
She never looked back. She never told all.

She dressed in silver, her hair was shining,
her walk was languid, and when she strolled the streets
bicyclists fell from their seats.

Nothing could offend her, no comment
slow her down, no friend would deny her,
no boundary could confine her.

And when she read her poems of longing
they jumped into the soul and each word sang.
Each languid phrase became a siren song.

The audience was thrilled and all afire.
For she was Gabriella Orvieto
and all she had was all that she desired.

Wickford

I miss yesterday and the luminous face
of my cornflower-blue sister as we walked
through the morning sea town, the white
Rose of Sharons by the roadside.

I miss the wind chimes that sang a perfect sonnet,
new yesterday, and the book left behind on the table
(never new again),

and the middle-aged man who rode by on his bike singing
that particular day, and how the old couple rowing
in their small dory were a kind of miracle,

and later how quiet the rain was in late afternoon, how
it licked like a summer cat while the black dog
slept on the cool tile
listening to the parsley and lemon balm hum.

Nereid Sister

I heard her opening her door
from her room below
in the windowless blue
studio just before sunrise,
the smell of chamomile lingering
from the nighttime dew.

How she slid into the water that dawn
she hardly remembered,
so much ouzo, so much sun
the day before.
I watched her climb down the rocky cliff
in the almost darkness
slipping out of her nightgown as out of a dream
and stepping into the crimson waves
while I guarded unseen
from the shadow of the cliff.

As her silver body, so like a girl's,
so like a nereid,
rose and dove, rose and dove
into the ripening Aegean,
her hair the color of starlight,
she was as free as I have ever seen her,
and full of a singing light.

She did not need
my protection after all
but still

I was glad
to have witnessed that beauty,
glad that she arose
like Venus and quietly ran back
to her gilded room.

My Father's Breath

*In the Greek church on the fortieth day after death, a memorial
service is said for the soul.*

It is forty days since your death. A hemisphere away,
I find the monastery of miracles,
Saint Rafael and Nicholas.

It is dusk, an amber sky.
We park the car quickly and I
run up the cobblestones to the door. Locked.

Too late to light a candle,
send you safely on,
as if I, your fallen angel, have the power,

as if you, stark Catholic, in heaven
already, would care about the forty days,
the candle lit.

Across the way is the church of the monastery,
The Church of Magadalene. The door is open.
A dark figure of a woman stands just inside.

She is chanting, but it is the sound of evening birds,
melodic, joyful. No death dirge. She will chant for hours,
incense of myrrh surrounding her.

No place to kneel, no chairs,
I stand before
the icon of Magdalene,

dark with age and sorrow,
tears pulsing behind my eyes,
and light my candle,

just as a breeze
blows a kiss
across the flame.
Amen.

Listen

In Mykonos there are no birds, but sea, and the sound
of wind
as it swims
through the open windows and the open blue shutters.
Nothing is green.
All is in the eye and the skin, the touch
and the taste
of salt, the clear line of rock against blue, the white square
houses, the white dotted hillsides of domes.
All is air and indigo and the whiteness of wind
blowing, blowing.

Outside the Monastery of Michael,
on the island of Lesvos,
the birds are carillons, an angelus,
the sound of a thousand bells, as if
every monk's page
turning in the dark cells
above us
has small cymbals,
each page ringing
against its silence.

As if all the leaves blowing outside the church
in the corridor
of green
sunlit shadows
on the stone wall where we sit
listening –
as if those leaves are brass

feathers in the wind
and all around, stillness

except for the birds

unseen, hidden,
hundreds and hundreds of green chimes,
singing,

singing.

Santorini Blue

On the cliffs of Santorini
she is measuring the blue
of sky, its parameters,
its immensity,
      where it turns white,
      where it dives down
            into the ancient caldera.
High above the small ships below,
all boundaries fall away.
There is only light
      and more light
            and the unmeasurable
silence.

She knows the coordinates
of her own life, the longitudes
and latitudes, her height,
her breadth. But it makes no sense
      to chart the expanse of blue
      as it makes no sense to count the years
            left, or the rain.
For now,
only this weightlessness,
      this cloudless
      universe
            holding her,
                arms sprung wide.

Woman in a Window

She sits above the pink oleander
as in a Vermeer,
gazing out past the harbor
to the ancient sea and sky.
The breeze from the dark Aegean
is caught in the blue square of window
and cools
her ageless face.
She takes the flowers from the zucchinis
and in the heat of the day,
spoonful by spoonful,
fills the petals with a melting sweetness
for us to taste.
There is no hurry.

We have rushed
down from the dry brown mountains,
full of rattles and chatter
of monasteries
and distant villages.
But she hears only
the ripple
of the sleeping
afternoon.

When the Turks Rode
into Smyrna

for Margo

In the hills of Smyrna
by the sunlit olive groves
they murdered your father
and then your mother,

your grandmother
and your aunt
near the giant washtub
where the silk garments
lay voiceless in the sun,
the lye burning the earth.

The children were hidden
in the cellars
of the great houses, with the wine
and the amphoras of oil
or sent to strange islands
in the early dawn
when the whispers began.

But your sister saw
them dragging your mother,
remembers
the screams,
and the burning of the house.
In old age,
she sees fires in her mirrors,
hears the cries.

You want to tell the story,
tell what you know,
what you heard,
what appears in your dreams
    but each time
        like Odysseus listening to the harper,
          it breaks your heart.

Shall We Walk the Narrow Streets of Mykonos?

On the outcropping of rock above the sea
we hear a plaintive, keening sound.
Mia says it is peacocks. I say it must be quail, who once lived
on the nearby island of Delos. Mia says, "No, it is peacocks.
Why don't you believe me?"

They cry like sad cats, of which there are many
on this small island. Perhaps in the winter the cats mate
with the peacocks, sailing their mournful sound
out through the wind in the summer.

Somewhere above my floating bed a dog
barks and below me the constant waves
soft as cashmere lap me to sleep.
A rooster crows earlier than dawn.
We have eaten rooster
and rabbit too, and silent large fish
and quail's eggs.
We have tanned our stomachs
and met as old people
at the bathroom at three in the morning
and slept after lunch and forgotten
lists and useless needs.

We are not as eternal as the small
white churches with their blue rounded roofs
that wander through the parched hills,
yellow with the sweet breath of camomile.
Here, one century dissolves into another, whole civilizations
fall into craters and are reborn, yet

we once thought we could sleep on the whitewashed
steps of this old church, forever sheltered from the wind,
and dance all night in the tavernas drinking retsina,
as far from the old women in black shawls
as from ancient Atlantis.

Cornwall

In stormy Cornwall
standing on the cliffs of Tintagel above a purple sea,
arms outstretched and joyous,
I remembered as if I had been there
a circle of women
in a pastel spring,
there before King Arthur, before the ruined castle fell,
perhaps as a sailor or a maiden,
or not even
that, but
a sheep
tinkling over the hillside,
a flower,
an asphodel, a buttercup
in some girl's hair,
a blade of wheat
in a ring of stones,
a piece of dust,
a spray of salt –
but there nonetheless,
a part of a canticle,
a singer in a ring
of dancers
holding back the gray sky above.

Encounter

I thought, Yes, I'll go to the Grand Canyon
yes, I'll go at dawn, no,
before first light,
no, first I will get up in the middle of the night and see
the wild pigs eating roots outside my window
next to stars the size of turnips
living among the trees of night.
And then I will go to the place at the edge of the canyon
in the darkness
to sit on the the rim
where my mother and uncle
and the brother
I never had, and my grandmother
and a wandering child will appear, as the light
lifts from the river,
and a white goddess with a red hawk's feather in her hair
will stand on the edge of the canyon
and lift herself above the rim
and fly into the cobalt morning light.

Block Island

The egg shaped hills
and the torn away bluffs,

the kettles in the hollows and the lazy hummocks,
the asters, the goldenrod,

the tombolos that connect the land
and the gullies winnowed in the wind,

the shallows and the rocky
cobbles, the drumlins

like giant earth bellies,
the berms and the bogs,

Cow Cove and Beach Plum Hill,
the chimneys rising beyond the round

curve of the porch,
and the tops of gables,

the path that disappears,
behind the hill,

the music unexpected
of the wind, of the sea,

the turning road,
the secret cove,

all that is hidden
all that is waiting.

Chrismal

In the back seat of the old Buick
leaving the city of New York at twilight,
I saw for the first time
the huge apartment houses,
the dark and starry rectangles along the highway,
thousands of spaces separate but collected,
each a neighborhood,
and for that moment, I knew the people in them.

Each person in those lighted windows had a soul like me
and skin and thoughts swirling and loving.
How many more worlds were there that I did not know?
How many children running in all their blushing colors,
kitchen lights hanging from ceilings, smells of cumin
and tarragon, chicken and pork and dumplings.

Each person in each apartment with pots,
each with a closet, a kitchen,
a hallway, and how many stairs? A window,
a vestibule perhaps, a longing, each
with jealousies
and fans in the summer, and
loneliness,

with great fears and light bulbs in their hallways,
an oil can for their car and forks and knives
as they sit down to dinner around the table,
one for each and all the forks and knives
of those twelve floors and then the twelve floors next
to the other and the other.
How much more was there that was not a part of me?

Inside me were trees and small roots
and houses of one floor or two
and one family lived in each, each with one roof.
Here, roofs extended for days,
even in the early evening,
and from so many rooms
lights softly simmered…
and in that light
some darkness lifted,
something slipped away.

When People Ask

Let it be said
that when the three young girls
of twenty
found that they were fifty
they went to Paris again,
drove the narrow roads of Provence
and smelled the lavender,

passed by the fields
of sunflowers
and felt the bright heat
of Van Gogh's sun.

Let it be said
that they backed down
one way streets
and knocked down many a sign,
that one went too fast, and one went too slow,
and one was always calm.

Let it be said that they did sit at Deux Garçons
under the plane trees across the wide boulevard
and listen to the cicadas,

that the days lasted long into the night
and fooled them with their light,

that everyday was new,
that Paris is forever young
and that still
the sight of the Seine at sunset
can make a young girl cry.

V. TWELVE MOONS

Twelve Moons

after Wallace Stevens

1

Half moon at Epiphany
Straight lined yin yang separating dark and light
On which side am I

2

The moon has its earthshine
Hanging on the birch
Watching each ice-covered branch

3

I learned on a day of no moon
That I am no Buddha
This is a new moon idea

4

I love the way you never lie
Clear as moonlight dark as thunder
I listen to your silent truths

5

I have resolved to make resolutions
The wise men knew how to follow
The star and say nothing

6

I have brought gifts – incense perfume gold
And returned along the same path
Pulling my mantle over my eyes and the eyes of the moon

7

The curve of the moon holds no fear
Though the stomach knows it like a body part
The back of the throat the inside of the knee

8

The crescent moon pretends never to grow old
Seems so content in its sliver of light
Daring the earth to draw a shadow

9

Rising above the trees the full moon
Hides even the stars
Snow covers every robin

10

One morning the moon closed with the sun rising
A cold jay flew up to the wire
Listening for the crackle of snow

11

One more moon in the night sky
To cast dreams upon new revelations
Lifting from within its mountains

12

Tonight the moon drinks the bay
Discovering the frozen waves
The way I will discover the day

Searching for Angels

In the distance silver foam crashes
against an invisible force,
a long white beard rising then disappearing
under the dark waves.

I take the windy path down to the pond
where it folds into goldenrod
and each rolling hill
loses itself in another.

The orange monarch outlined in her black coat
forgets
that not long ago,
in a night of infinite stars she turned
her world inside out and flew.

I cannot lose myself like the gentle hills
or the quiet snake who sheds his skin and moves on.
I can only take my boat out among
the white lilies, balancing somewhere
between earth and sky, searching for angels.

Lazy Girl

August is a long,
    slim-armed, lazy girl
doing a languid backstroke in the bay
    or paddling through canyons
of salt grass, listening
    for migrations and the sound
Monarchs make on the last purple flower.
    She slips in and out
    of warmth as the days grow shorter,
her fuschia mouth
    opening like fishes
and closing like the dying Queen Anne's lace.

September

September is a melody I know
that lingers sharp as salt on the lips
and sings the door closed. It empties chairs
and flings the blown toys across the sand.
It strikes lightning and swells the rushing sea.

It is a bright moon glowing like a clock
ticking and one tree turning inside out.
It is the sound of leaves clinging
against the rusty wind. It is beauty
and sorrow and the clanking bones of trees
that watch as the stars grow brighter.

Autumnal Equinox in Vermont

Why I plant anything called Fake Sunflower
is a mystery and yet I have planted them
willy-nilly on a little hillside that is not a planting
bed but looks down a few yards to a trickling
swamp-like stream and beyond into the woods
where sunlight peers in straight lines through the trees.
The fake sunflowers will surely be eaten by deer or bear
or tawny mountain lions as were the hibiscus
I planted last month, but for now they willow in their
   golden space.

In the local supermarket I meet my former neighbor
who does not recognize me at first and who
at 91 is mourning the fact that he cannot
do as much weeding as he used to. He keeps at it though.
He turns as I do in the autumnal light, feeling the balance
of the earth, the twirling sundial, the final day
of summer, each moment diaphanous.

I buy the Cinderella pumpkin though it is more expensive
than the rest, along with the "we-grow-it-ourselves"
corn and the gourds that look like distorted fairy godmothers'
crowns with stripes and swirls like circling planets.
Time is divided evenly today, seeping
through the turning leaves.
Soon the darkness and silence will begin.
The bear will appear in the night sky
lumbering into his sky cave. The white rabbit will slip
here and there.

The bear will think he has you in his cave. He won't have you.
The sky will be more luminous. You will see more clearly.
There will be more wonder now the time is past for butterflies.

Harlequin

October, so glad to be here, so ready to be gone,
your falling pears heaving
with the weight that breaks boughs.
Oh October, you counterfeit spring, you masquerader,
so bright and shining yet all about going,
all about the last of things,
the final shimmering glimpse of the Dipper before
Orion cudgels in, his belt ready
to swing through the winter sky.
The tender purple asters are here and then gone too
but still, your yellow mirrors,
your golden baskets of sun spill
over us like a Harlequin's smile
and for awhile we forget you are a jester.

Winter Solstice

This is no ordinary time.
Reindeer
climb the skies,
fires
light the hillsides
and the bear comes in.

The air is sharp
and the sky is more
transparent now. Prayers travel easily through it.
From where we are we can see the Universe
just beginning.

From where we are
new islands are appearing,
the bare
trees
are sterling and gold.

In the shining cold
we hide under the covers
as though
spring will never return. But watch

how the earth tilts towards the sun,
swinging
in its spinning
blue space.

Watch how the light

chases the darkness,
the lilting stars
expand
and slide into morning.

Let's gather the winter colors around,
spin them
into magical white,
lean into the earth
and bend with it.
The dark sky will open.

The Uncleared Paths

All anticipation past,
the snows arrive
without premeditation

beautiful beyond thought,
rounding sculptures everywhere.
Dark light above the blue white barn

whispers secret songs of freedom
to the black dog only he can hear.
The stark moon rises

riding a white dagger cloud,
lights the black jagged branches of the apple tree.
There are angels in the snow in shapes of children

and odd forms of harmony. No one
is outside but me and the dog and the snow.
The tilting wind surges through the pines

from Canada or Siberia or the Russian steppes.
It speaks of loss and the impossible
though still we walk

the orphaned, uncleared paths,
sure that the tangled light will return
despite all logic.

February

February is not flirtatious.
She is cold and brilliant,
calculating and steadfast.
She knows hers is the last
certainty, the last absolute
darkness
      between darknesses.

In the days she has left
she flings her glittering hair
over the black lines of trees,
breaking boughs as she sings,
her voice the cry of geese keening
"yesterday, yesterday."

VI. WHAT GIVES THE HEART EASE

Once Again

I am going to take a vow of silence
and listen to spring coming,
listen to the snow whispering away
into the morning sky,
to the waves receding and pulling forth,
hear the creaking dock and the wind
that sounds like evergreens.
I am going to listen to the hiss
of the welcome heat
rising from the dark cellar,
and the hush of the tablecloth
descending to the table.
I will listen for the quiet
sound of your whistling,
the wrinkle of your laughter, the glide
of your shirt and slide of your shoes,
the clink of ice in the glass, the fork
on the porcelain plate,
the sound of the world together
unbroken by words.

Their Wings Transparent

As trees go, the silver birch does not live long
but surely will outlive me,
planted as it was when I was twenty.

I watch its bird-shaped seeds
in summer sail on every surface.
I find them on my clothes and in my bed,

in pages of a book just opened,
their wings transparent,
thinner than a butterfly's.

It seems impossible that they should grow,
indiscriminate as they are, so careless where they sail,
with whom they sleep.

If I could I would grow them in my hair,
or become myself a catkin, then the tree
growing tall and legendary,

roots deep and watered,
glancing without questions
up towards heaven.

White Birch

Say the white birch, taller than the house
and losing leaves from broken branches,
say it is polished silver, more beautiful
with time. Say it is more beautiful to be old,
like sea glass or shells made into glittering sand.
Say the sunflower hanging over the branch of the crabapple
as its petals darken and drop, the pears
ripening on the tree, say they are becoming,
not diminished, only loosening their ties to the bough.

The Voice of Water

Through the threshold of two shining birches
I find the vernal pool.
Five trees hang on its edge,
as if the pool had just been created,
filled by the great storm
and the trees trying to find their balance.
Beneath me the ground tilts
as I try to unfold my chair.

Just sit.
Do not bring chairs or writing pad
or camera.
Listen.

Rings, spirals, ripples appear
without sound or bird or fallen leaf to cause them.
You may do it all. Yes.

On the water perfect twins of trees and clouds
widen the unmoving sky. The air is silent
Yes, she answers again   and   again.

What Gives the Heart Ease

The sea, beyond the small pine,
the brave winging of tiny birds
on this cold, bright morning,
the great blue heron
rising from the marsh
into the quicksilver sky,
clouds glowing like mountains,
the scallop shell, mussel, clam and oyster broken
and shining on the beach
but not broken by longing.

What ache I feel at your kindness,
at the bell sound of a single bird
in a distant tree. Though wounds
stay and glitter like the winter moon
the heart is calmed by the simple
cleansing of the waves, the songs
of the hidden world, your voice.

Flight

The white sun pulls against
the dark sky, and shadow
of geese flying south falls
over me as they ascend
higher and higher
beyond the cairn of rock
and shallow pool.

I am cradled and held here
like a motionless wave,
but dreaming of a song of going

where one day soars above another,
each day more weightless,
each day a melody,
a prayer
against the pressing sky

until I am no longer shadow, or dust
or aimless wind
but shining and silver
free as the sea, washed clean
and slipping from the old skin,
unfolding like rain, unfolding
like stars, like whirlpools of light into
a dance of joy
beyond darkness.

The Chambered Nautilus

Everything that spirals, lightens
and spills light,
Milky Way, conch, daisy, and sand dune,
caterpillar, galaxy, sunflower,
apple seed, rope,
concerto,

children spinning from the womb
somersaulting into life,
jazz trombones and ballerinas, aching stars,
the fiddlehead fern and the cowslip, the wheel whirling
   to the market,
the core of wood and a woodpecker's back, the belly,
the eye of the seagull, the eye of the bee,

arguments and truths and seekers, all spiraling, all rising
and falling back, rolling inside and out –
all waterfall, and cyclone
only to grow lighter with each turning,
as when we walk the labyrinth, closing off the old chambers
to float in the buoyant air of the journey.

May I Suggest

from Susan Werner's song with the same title

May I suggest
this is the best day of your life
with the water warm and blue, and the wind
pulling the sky through the door where
the wind chimes are singing
and the dog has had a bath and is as cool
as he's been all day.
May I suggest that the stones on the beach have never
been so beautiful
nor the basil so plentiful.
Each morning I listen for the gulls
or the mockingbird, for the sound
of the paper in the air and the garbage man
who is always happy.
At night the thunder ricochets
across the Sound for hours
and still the white hibiscus
blossoms against the dark sky.

The Source

The lakes
long to stay in stillness
glistening,

contained,
closed.
But time does not let them.

Drawn down they are pulled
tumbling from the dark mountain,
becoming the river:
Source, Dancer, Singer.

We feel it in our liquid bodies,
the quality of water slipping through us,
spinning sand, carrying birth bone,
mirror,
the salt of tears.

Restless, hurried,
the river winds, makes canyons,
whistles over jagged rocks,
turns, rushes, gathers,

then
finally, slowing,
grows wider, flows deeper,

seeks the ancient music,
seeks the sea beyond,

without, within.

The Hudson

That the great river begins
in these mountains
is hardly known.
Hidden high above is a silent pool,
a small tarn the shape of a tear,
and here
it begins.
To arrive there you must cross
the Opalescent River
which shimmers in the rimming clouds.
No one else
will be there.
The sky overpowers
the path and the land overpowers
us. In this wilderness one asks
what it is we are meant to do,
here where the long cliffs
drop from the sky.
What is it we have not seen,
green as we are,
of beginnings,
of our own undiscovered lands?

Found

In the deep
breathless sigh
of the forest
our son moves
below us
like a gazelle,
like a sail as we descend

into the valley
of the giant redwoods.
It is late afternoon in a cold April.
There is the threat of rain and we
are traveling an unmarked trail,
the usual bridge
covered
in rushing waters.

He disappears below us in the circles of greenness.

We follow the path
like a labyrinth, whose end we cannot know.
I turn to see the way back
and stumble, as the sky disappears.
There is no sound.

Our breath quickens as we go lower.
My feet sink in the softness of moss,
a feeling of floating as in deep,
leafy waters,
the silence of being

underground.
I whistle. No answer.

Finally in the distance we see the grove,
the elders, the giant ones,
the tallest of all sentinels, immense beyond logic,
detached, quiet, holy.
Our son sits below the tallest, like a Buddha.

I move forward, touch
the tree's velvet skin, feel a vibration
as in a hum of waves thousands of miles away,
one
harmonious note,
dispelling all fear,
circling through eons and eons
of years,
like stars.

ABOUT THE AUTHOR

Lana Orphanides taught English and Creative Writing at New London High School for eighteen years. She received advanced degrees from Northeastern University and Wesleyan University and is the author of *Sea and the Sound of Wind, Poems of Greece*, as well as a collaborative book of poetry and paintings, *Spring: Rebirth and Renewal*. She has been the opening voice at the Arts Café Mystic, the featured poet in the Hygienic Poetry Series and also in the Hidden Treasures Poetry Series at the Courtyard Gallery. In addition, her poetry was part of a multimedia exhibition at the Alexey von Schlippe Gallery. She is a member of the Connecticut River Poets and Cerebellum, a group which gives workshops combining art, poetry, and dance. Lana was recently nominated for The Pushcart Prize. With her husband, Dimi, she lives in Groton, Connecticut, on Pine Island Bay, a continual source of inspiration.

This book is set in Garamond Premier Pro, which had its genesis in 1988 when type-designer Robert Slimbach visited the Plantin-Moretus Museum in Antwerp, Belgium, to study its collection of Claude Garamond's metal punches and typefaces. During the mid-fifteen hundreds, Garamond—a Parisian punch-cutter—produced a refined array of book types that combined an unprecedented degree of balance and elegance, for centuries standing as the pinnacle of beauty and practicality in type-founding. Slimbach has created an entirely new interpretation based on Garamond's designs and on compatible italics cut by Robert Granjon, Garamond's contemporary.

To order additional copies of this book
or other Antrim House titles, contact the publisher at

Antrim House
21 Goodrich Rd., Simsbury, CT 06070
860.217.0023, AntrimHouse@comcast.net
or the house website (www.AntrimHouseBooks.com).

•

On the house website
in addition to information on books
you will find sample poems, upcoming events,
and a "seminar room" featuring supplemental biography,
notes, images, poems, reviews, and
writing suggestions.